Achieving Your Goals in 2025: A Christmas-Inspired Systematic Approach

Swaroop Singh

Published by Swaroop singh, 2024.

ACHIEVING YOUR GOALS IN 2025: A CHRISTMAS-INSPIRED SYSTEMATIC APPROACH

First edition. December 28, 2024.

Copyright © 2024 Swaroop Singh.

ISBN: 979-8230705772

Written by Swaroop Singh.

Table of Contents

Christmas time reminds us that miracles are possible when we open our hearts and align our actions with love and gratitude. Let this season be your opportunity to manifest joy and blessings—not just for yourself, but for everyone around you.

Faith is the essence of manifestation. When you believe in the possibility of joy, blessings, and miracles, you open yourself to endless opportunities. This Christmas, let your faith be the guide that transforms challenges into celebrations and desires into reality.Remember, the power to manifest lies within you—trust it, nurture it, and watch the magic unfold.

This Christmas, let gratitude be your guiding principle. Appreciate the blessings around you, visualize your desires with gratitude, and trust that the universe is working in your favor. The more you practice gratitude, the more miracles you will experience

Setting intentions transforms the holiday season from a series of tasks into a meaningful experience. It empowers you to focus on what matters, stay on track, navigate challenges with grace, and manifest joy and blessings.

When you align your thoughts, feelings, and actions with your intentions, you become a magnet for the experiences and energy you desire. Whether it's peace, connection, or abundance, the power of intention ensures that your holiday season is purposeful and fulfilling.

Let your intentions for this season bring you immense joy, love, and blessings.

Visualization transforms your thoughts, emotions, and energy, helping you create a joyful Christmas filled with love and abundance. It empowers you to focus on what truly matters, navigate challenges gracefully, and manifest meaningful experiences.

When you visualize with clarity and emotion, you align yourself with the spirit of the season, allowing joy, love, and blessings to flow effortlessly into your life.

Chapter Index for "Achieving Your Goals in 2025: A Systematic Approach"

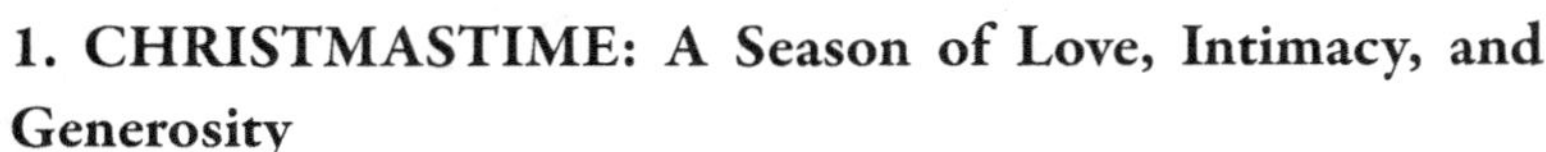

1. CHRISTMASTIME: A Season of Love, Intimacy, and Generosity

- Christmastime as a Symbol of Hope and Renewal
- The Power of Intention in Manifestation
- Clara's Christmastime Wish: A Story of Gratitude

2. The Power of Belief in Manifestation

- Assumption as the Core of Manifestation
- Shifting Mindset Through Faith
- Enhancing Resilience with Belief

3. APPRECIATION AS a Tool for Manifestation

- The Science Behind Gratitude
- Shifting Perspective from Lack to Abundance
- Gratitude Rituals for Daily Practice

4. Setting Intentions for the Season

- Reflecting on Personal Values
- Using Positive Language to Set Intentions
- Practical Exercises for Intention Setting

5. VISUALIZING A HAPPY Christmastime

- Steps for Effective Visualization
- The Role of Emotion in Manifestation
- Visualization Exercises and Techniques

6. SHARING LOVE AND Kindness

- Acts of Kindness: Transforming Lives
- Building Stronger Relationships with Generosity
- Challenges and How to Overcome Them

7. PRACTICAL ACTIVITIES for Sharing Love and Kindness

- Journaling Prompts to Inspire Generosity
- Acts of Generosity Challenge
- Visualization Exercises to Amplify Love

8. CARRYING THE SPIRIT of Christmastime Throughout the Year

- Proof as a Year-Round Practice
- Creating Rituals Inspired by Festive Values
- Overcoming Challenges to Maintain Generosity

CHAPTER 1:
CHRISTMASTIME
A SEASON OF
LOVE INTIMACY
AND
GENEROSITY

Christmastime Is More Than Just A Festive Season

Christmastime is more than just a festive season, it is an opportunity for affection, intimacy, and heartfelt empathy. It symbolizes hope, renewal, and the boundless potential of love and generosity. The essence of Christmastime lies in its ability to inspire us to reflect on the blessings in our lives, cherish our relationships, and spread joy to others.

Exhibiting joy and blessings during Christmastime means aligning our hopes, emotions, and actions with the positive energy that this season represents. It is about creating the experiences we desire by embodying gratitude, love, and the power of intention.

THE POWER OF INTENTION in Christmastime **Manifestation**

Manifestation begins with a clear intention. When you set an intention for what you wish to experience or give during Christmas—be it happiness, peace, or abundance—you direct your energy toward making it a reality. Christmastime is the perfect moment to practice this, as the season naturally brings an atmosphere of hope and anticipation.

The Tale of Clara's Christmastime Wish

Clara, a single mother, wanted to give her children a memorable Christmas despite her financial challenges. Instead of dwelling on what she lacked, Clara decided to focus on manifesting joy.

She wrote down her intentions: to fill her home with love, laughter, and a few simple but meaningful gifts for each child.

Clara practiced daily gratitude for the blessings she already had—her health, her children, and the support of friends. She visualized her children opening presents and enjoying a cozy Christmas meal. Her positive mindset attracted unexpected support:

A neighbor shared decorations.

A local charity donated gifts.

A friend invited them to a festive dinner.

Clara's Christmas turned out even more magical than she had imagined.

Applying This to Your Life

Like Clara, you can manifest your best Christmastime by following these steps:

1. Setting Clear Intentions

Define what you want to feel and experience this Christmas. Because these background clear intention method lays out how you are going to feel and what you want to do this Christmas.

Cleanliness leads to the importance of purpose and meaningful feasting.

2. Practicing Gratitude

Devote effort to something the blessings you then have and recognize them seriously Undertaking gratitude includes accepting and appreciating the advantages you earlier have. This heartfelt practice supports eagerness, joy, and a deeper links to the festival spirit..

3. Taking Inspired Action

Act small acts of generosity, embellish your space, or constitute genuine gifts.Communicable stimulated action resources charming in meaningful projects like acts of generosity, decorating your room, or crafting genuine aptitude to spread love and cheer this season.

4. Trusting in Surprises

Trust that your exertions and positive strength will entice blessings.Trustful in surprises resources believing that your zeal and exertions will interest unexpected approvals. This trust invites appearance and wonder into your Christmas parties.

<u>Christmastime reminds us that miracles are possible when we open our hearts and align our actions with love and gratitude. Let this season be your opportunity to manifest joy and blessings—not just for yourself, but for everyone around you</u>.

CHAPTER 2: THE POWER OF BELIEF IN MANIFESTATION

Assumption As The Core Of Manifestation

Assumption is the foundation of all manifestation. It is the hidden force shaping our concepts, emotions, and actions, transforming our deepest desires into reality. Without belief, even the most powerful intentions lack the strength to materialize.

When we truly trust in something, we align ourselves with its frequency and draw it into our lives.

In the context of Christmas and the festive season, faith takes on even greater importance. Christmas is a time when belief, hope, and miracles are celebrated. From childhood tales of Santa Claus to the spiritual ideals of goodwill, the season encourages us to trust in the extraordinary.

This faith fuels the magic of the season and reminds us of the power within ourselves to create joy and blessings.

What is Belief in Manifestation?

Belief in manifestation is the unwavering trust that what you desire will come to fruition. It involves:

1. Unshakable Certainty:

Knowing in your heart that your goal is achievable and your unwavering determination is the unwavering belief that your goal is attainable, deeply embedded in your soul. This confidence promotes flexibility, clarity, and focused functioning..

2. Emotional Alignment:

Feeling joy and enthusiasm as if your desire has already manifested and thus enthusiastic alignment is to soak yourself in the effects of happiness, excitement and accomplishment, as if your goal has already been achieved. This appeals to positive affects.

3. Aligned Action:

Aligned action involves taking purposeful, meaningful steps that resonate with your belief in achieving your goal. It bridges the gap between intention and manifestation.

Manifestation operates on the Law of Attraction: you attract what you believe in and invest energy into. When you trust wholeheartedly, your mind becomes focused, your emotions powerful, and your actions intentional, setting off a chain of events that brings your desires closer to reality.

How Assumption Influences Manifestation

1. Shifts Your Mindset:

Faith Helps You Transition From Doubt To Confidence. A strong belief system prevents negative thoughts and fears from overwhelming your goals. For instance, when you trust that you can find happiness during Christmas despite challenges, your mind actively seeks reasons to be joyful and ways to create cheer.

2. Activates the Subconscious Mind:

Your subconscious mind plays a pivotal role in manifestation. It doesn't distinguish between reality and imagination. When you believe deeply, your subconscious accepts your vision as real and aligns your thoughts, emotions, and actions to achieve it.

3. Enhances Resilience:

Challenges are inevitable, but faith keeps you moving forward. It fuels perseverance and motivates you to overcome obstacles, ensuring you stay focused on your desires.

4. Amplifies Vibrational Energy:

Everything in the universe is energy, including thoughts and emotions. Faith generates a high-frequency vibration that aligns with your desires, making them more likely to manifest.

A FAMILY'S CHRISTMAS MIRACLE

The Johnson family faced financial hardships one Christmas. They couldn't afford lavish decorations or gifts. Yet, they believed in the spirit of the season. They decorated their home with handmade ornaments, sang carols, and wrote notes of gratitude to one another.

Their faith in joy and togetherness created a warm, loving atmosphere. Their neighbor, moved by their enthusiasm, gifted them a box of treats. A local charity donated toys for the children. The Johnsons experienced a Christmas filled with love and kindness, proving that faith can bring unexpected blessings.

A PERSONAL GOAL MANIFESTED

Emily longed to mend her relationship with her estranged sister during Christmas. She believed in forgiveness and reconciliation. She wrote her sister a heartfelt letter and visualized them celebrating together.

Despite initial doubts, Emily's faith gave her the courage to act. To her surprise, her sister responded positively, and they reconciled over Christmas dinner. Emily's belief in healing paved the way for a renewed bond.

STEPS TO STRENGTHEN YOUR FAITH

1. Set a Clear Goal:

Figure out what you want to manifest. You must define the outcome you want, a happy Christmas period that you desire, imperfectly. Specific objectives provide management and form the basis for certification.

For example, "I want to experience a joyful, peaceful Christmas with loved ones."

2. Visualize Daily:

Spend a few minutes each day imagining your desire as if it has already come true. Picture the smiles, laughter, and festive atmosphere.

3. Practice Gratitude:

Appreciation reinforces the idea you are already focusing on. A grateful essence invites more blessings. Connect with visualizing your goal as already achieved. Embrace the emotions, atmosphere, and significance to strengthen the principle and align with your desired sensibility

4. Replace Doubt:

Transform doubts into affirmations. Instead of saying, "This might not happen," say, "I trust that this will happen."

Appreciation shifts focus to what you have, constituting a definite psychology. This openmindedness promotes the flow of sanctifications and supports your proof process.

5. Surround Yourself with Positivity:

Engage with people who uplift you and strengthen your belief in possibilities. Avoid negativity, as it weakens your faith.

Scientific Perspective On Faith And Manifestation

Psychologists and neuroscientists have found that belief significantly impacts our behavior and outcomes.

The Placebo Effect is a powerful example: patients who believe they are receiving effective treatment often improve, even when the treatment is inactive. This demonstrates the mind's ability to influence reality through faith.

Similarly, visualization and positive thinking activate the brain's Reticular Activating System (RAS), which filters information and helps you notice opportunities aligned with your desires. For instance, if you believe you'll have a fulfilling Christmas, you'll naturally notice moments of joy, opportunities for connection, and reasons to celebrate.

HARNESSING THE POWER of Faith This Christmas

1. Believe in Joy:

Even if circumstances seem challenging, trust that you can create happiness. Engage in activities that bring joy, like baking, decorating, or spending time with loved ones.

2. Believe in Miracles:

Allow yourself to dream big. Whether it's reconciliation, abundance, or peace, trust that the season's magic can make it happen.

3. Inspire Others:

Share your faith in the goodness of the season. Acts of kindness, uplifting conversations, and a cheerful attitude can inspire those around you.

A Practical Exercise: The Christmas Manifestation Journal

1. Label three meaningful wishes for this Christmas time, whether emotional, material or practical. Writing down the rule square gives clarity and focus to your exposition.

2. Art Confidence Affirmations affirm your talent to achieve every desire. These beneficial affirmations align your mindset with your goals, empowering willful action and performance

For example:

Desire: "I want a joyful Christmas."

Belief: "I believe I can create joy by appreciating the small moments."

3. Regular praise reinforces a supportive psychology, while engaging intentional steps bridge the gap between desire and existence. This habit fosters focus and progress.

CONCLUSION:

Faith is the essence of manifestation. When you believe in the possibility of joy, blessings, and miracles, you open yourself to endless opportunities. This Christmas, let your faith be the guide that transforms challenges into celebrations and desires into reality.Remember, the power to manifest lies within you—trust it, nurture it, and watch the magic unfold.

CHAPTER 3:
APPRECIATION AS A TOOL FOR MANIFESTATION

The Power of Gratitude

Appreciation is one of the most powerful tools for manifestation. It is the practice of recognizing and valuing the blessings in your life, no matter how small or abundant they may seem. Gratitude shifts your focus from lack to abundance, creating a positive energy that aligns with the frequency of what you want to manifest.

WHEN YOU EXPRESS APPRECIATION, you communicate to the universe, "I am ready to receive more." This mindset opens the door for greater blessings to flow into your life. Appreciation acts as a magnet, attracting positive experiences, people, and opportunities that resonate with your goals.

WHAT IS APPRECIATION in Manifestation?

Appreciation in manifestation goes beyond simply saying "thank you." It is a deep, sincere recognition of:

1. What You Already Have:

Acknowledging your current blessings strengthens the energy of abundance, inviting more positivity and prosperity into your existence by focusing on the appreciation and enjoyment of what you already have.

2. What You Are Manifesting:

Feeling grateful for your desires already, as if they have already become reality. Such exposure means expressing gratitude as if your desires have already been fulfilled, aligning your stimuli with the sensitivity you desire, and creating a certain mindset that attracts what you really want..

<u>By focusing on appreciation, you elevate your vibrational frequency to align with what you want to attract. It strengthens your belief, enhances your energy, and fosters a sense of alignment with your goals</u>

THE SCIENCE BEHIND Appreciation and Manifestation

Gratitude is not just a spiritual concept; it has scientific backing:

1. Activates Positive Hormones:

Gratitude activates the release of "feel good" chemicals called dopamine and serotonin, which promote happiness and satisfaction. These projectiles as weapons improve mood, reduce stress, and support a sense of well-being. Regular appreciation helps to relieve some frustrations, leading to better health. It strengthens emotional resilience, motivates individuals to better cope with challenges, and creates better prospects in life. By attracting what we like, we invite more positivity and happiness into our lives..

2. REWIRES THE BRAIN:

Regular gratitude practices reshape neural pathways, making your brain more attuned to positive thoughts and experiences. By holding on to what we are generally good at, we train our brains to naturally notice and acknowledge the good in history. This shift helps reinforce overall prosperity and supports a mindset that thrives on enthusiasm, creating a stage of appreciation that leads to satisfaction and sensitive elasticity.

3. Strengthens the Reticular Activating System (RAS):

Appreciation programs the Reticular Stimulating Method (RAS) in your brain, that arrange filtering news and concentrating on what's most influential. By undertaking gratitude, you train your RAS to devote effort to something belongings that align accompanying your aims, making you more aware of freedom that support your desires. This profound awareness helps you notice event for exhibition, as your brain prioritizes helpful, goal-oriented hopes and occurrences.

Recognition programs the Troublesome Activating Plan (RAS) in your intelligence by influencing the habit you see and devote effort to something certain provocation. The RAS is a network of neurons situated in the brainstem, responsible for penetrating and prioritizing sonic news, directing your consideration to what is most appropriate or important. It acts like a watchperson, determining that information gets pass on to the alert brain for deeper prepare.

When you practice recognition and gratitude, you basically educate your mind to recognize and devote effort to something certain experiences, community, and belongings. Recognition signals to your RAS that these positive details are important, increasing your knowledge of ruling class in your routine life.

E.g., if you express recognition for kindness or advantage, your RAS enhances informed about latest trends to noticing those features in the globe around you. Over occasion, this think about closely embellishes your ability to visualize convenience, solutions, and readiness, frequently revamping your outlook on existence.

The RAS functions by emphasize what is in alignment accompanying your current psychology or spirits. By consistently charming in recognition, you shift your mental state toward readiness and exposure.

This, in proper sequence, encourages your RAS to pierce more of what you acknowledge, whether it's love, fame, or even limited acts of generosity. As a result, the more you enjoy, the more you strengthen positive understanding patterns, growing feelings of pleasure, comfort, and appreciation.In summary, appreciation not only improves your impassioned well-being but likewise programs your RAS to devote effort to something the helpful aspects of history. This strong connection 'tween concept and idea helps you manifest a life suffused accompanying gratitude and affluence.

How Appreciation Enhances Manifestation

1. Shifts Your Perspective:

Appreciation shifts your focus from what you don't have. This positive attitude attracts more abundance.

By focusing on the positive aspects of your life, you shift your mindset from lack to abundance. This shift helps create a more positive and grateful attitude, which in turn attracts more blessings and opportunities. When you recognize the value of what you already have, you open yourself up to receiving even more. This practice of appreciating what you have strengthens your connection to abundance and increases your ability to manifest more of it in your life.

2. Raises Your Vibration:

Manifestation works on the law of energy alignment. Gratitude raises your vibration to a frequency that matches your desires, increasing the likelihood of manifestation.

Gratitude plays a key role in this process by raising your vibration to a greater frequency. When you express gratitude, you bring more of what you are grateful for, connecting your strength with the frequency of your desires. This increase in supportive power makes it easier to manifest your desires. By expressing gratitude generally, you increase your strength, as well as the likelihood of manifesting the history and experiences you undoubtedly want.

3. Strengthens Your Belief:

When you feel grateful for your blessings, you develop a deep trust in the universe's ability to give. This trust increases the power of your intentions. It infuses your thoughts with readiness. Appreciation opens the door to receiving more, as it shifts your focus from what you already have to what you don't have. It strengthens your connection with outer space, improving your manifestation skills. By practicing gratitude, you establish a flow of prosperity and bring more blessings into your existence, reinforcing your belief that outer space is constantly on your side.

4. Creates Emotional Alignment:

Appreciation creates feelings of joy, love, and satisfaction, which are crucial for connecting with the energy of what you want to manifest. When you express sincere appreciation, you vibrate at a symmetry that invites more supportive energy into your history. These feelings help you connect deeply with your desires, energizing your focus and goals. The act of appreciation also nurtures a mindset of abundance, making it easier to manifest the present style you want.

By nurturing recognition, you connect your passionate energy with your goals, generating a powerful flow of attraction that supports the fulfillment of your goals.

<u>Examples of Appreciation as a Tool for Manifestation</u>
Example 1: Manifesting Financial Abundance
Elon struggled to manage his finances. Instead of focusing on his debts, he started a gratitude journal, listing things he was thankful for: a stable job, supportive family, and small achievements like paying bills on time.

Over time, his mindset shifted from scarcity to abundance. His gratitude opened his mind to new opportunities. He received a promotion, discovered ways to save money, and even started a side business. Elon's financial situation improved significantly because gratitude helped him align with abundance.

Example 2: Manifesting Better Relationships
Maria wanted a closer bond with her partner. Instead of dwelling on their disagreements, she began appreciating the positive

aspects of their relationship: shared laughter, mutual support, and cherished memories.

Her gratitude created a loving atmosphere, encouraging her partner to reciprocate. They started communicating better and spending more quality time together. Maria's relationship transformed because her appreciation fostered love and understanding.

Practical Steps to Use Appreciation for Manifestation

1. Start a Gratitude Journal:

Write down five things you are grateful for each day, including both current blessings and what you are manifesting.

Example: "I am grateful for my loving family."

Example: "I am thankful for the new job opportunity coming my way."

---

2. FEEL IT DEEPLY:

Don't just list your blessings—immerse yourself in the feelings of gratitude. Experience the joy, love, and appreciation as you write or reflect on your blessings.

Immersing yourself in gratitude means deeply feeling joy, love, and appreciation for your blessings. It's not just listing them but truly connecting with the emotions they bring, amplifying positivity and attracting more reasons to feel grateful.

3. Express Gratitude in Advance:

The "Manifest Your Desires Already" resources demonstrate the psychology, emotions, and behaviors associated with achieving your goals as if they are already real, which is the path to attracting and manifesting success at the event..

Example: If you are manifesting a new home, say, "I am so thankful for my beautiful, cozy home."

4. USE AFFIRMATIONS:

Repeat appreciation-based affirmations over and over again to connect thoughts with curiosity in your subconscious mind, develop a mindset of appreciation, and a deeper connection to love, generosity, and all aspects of history.

Example: "I am grateful for the abundance that flows into my life effortlessly."

Example: "I am thankful for all the blessings, seen and unseen."

5. Practice Gratitude in Action:

Express your gratitude through meaningful behavior like helping someone with a share of something, giving back to society, or simply saying "thank you." These simple but effective gestures show your gratitude and encourage generosity, strengthen relationships, and spread curiosity to those around you.

Daily Gratitude Ritual

Here's a simple daily routine to integrate gratitude into your manifestation practice:

1. Morning Reflection:

Start your life by listing three things you enjoy when you wake up in the morning. This practice creates a positive atmosphere for your life, connects your thoughts with appreciation and joy, helps you strive for something good in life, and maintains a psychology of love, kindness, and readiness..

2. Visualization with Gratitude:

Give 5 records while imagining your desires as if they have already been fulfilled. While imagining, feel deep appreciation for having them. This exercise helps you connect your strengths with your goals, improving your opinion and expression ability. Appreciation enhances positive empathic guidance to your desires, making it easier for bureaucracy to manifest in sensitivity..

3. Evening Journaling:

Evening diary involves thinking about your day, including writing down the blessings you have experienced. This practice helps you acknowledge the positive moments in your life. Additionally, write about feeling one step closer to your goal, as this encourages progress and mindfulness. This process promotes gratitude, focus, and motivation to achieve your objectives.

Challenges and How to Overcome Them

1. Struggling to Find Gratitude During Difficult Times:

Solution: Start small. Focus on basic blessings like health, shelter, or a kind gesture from a stranger. Gratitude grows with practice.

When facing challenging times, it can be troublesome to find reasons to feel nice. The key to beating this struggle search out start limited. In the midst of situation, putting on elementary advantages to a degree your health, shelter, or even entity as plain as a kind action from a outsider can help shift your focus from what is going wrong to what is going right.

Frequently, all the while hard times, we enhance focused on the negative facets of our position, that only deepens feelings of incompetence and disappointment.

Nevertheless, the act of concentrating on natural, everyday sanctifications can start to open your soul to impressions of recognition.

Health is a essential advantage, frequently implicit just before it is challenged. If you are concerning matter well, namely previously a important advantage to feel thankful for. Likewise, bearing a ceiling over your head, nevertheless by means of what humble, determines shelter from the harshness of the globe.

These are fundamental facets of existence that frequently go ignored but deserve acknowledgment all the while troublesome periods.Another strong tool is understanding narrow acts of generosity. A smirk from a newcomer, a helping hand from a companion, or even a importance of joint amusement can prod us that there is still excellence in the realm.

These acts, though limited, can lift our morale and support a sense of connection, lowering impressions of seclusion and despair.Appreciation evolves with practice. By making it a clothing to recognize not completely individual item expected grateful each era, even in tough class, you will evenly build a psychology of gratitude. Over occasion, this shift in view will not only help you deal with troublesome periods but also improve your overall sense of happiness.

2. Doubting the Process:

Solution: Remind yourself of past instances where gratitude led to positive outcomes. Maintain faith in the process.

Resolution of "Questioning the Process":Doubt often stands when next results are not visible, inducing restraint. Nevertheless, the key to overcoming this display or take public trustful the process of gratitude and remembering allure substantiated benefits.

Begin by indicating on past instances place practicing appreciation caused certain outcomes in your growth. Plan importance when expressing appreciation enhanced your mood, friendships, or overall sense of welfare.

This practice helps prod you of the power appreciation holds and convinces you that it works over period, not directly.Conviction is another crucial item. Learn that the process of gratitude is a step-by-step individual, and allure effects expand accompanying consistency. A suggestion of correction concentrating on which you lack, channel your energy into being appreciative for that reason you already have.

Appreciation supports a definite mindset, that brings more bounty into your life.Individual active way to persist path search out maintain a appreciation chronicle.

Write down three belongings regularly that you are appreciative for, no matter by what method limited they may appear. This clothing helps strengthen positive thinking and serves as a record of the approvals in your growth. Revisit this chronicle all the while importance of doubt to regain assurance in the process.Furthermore, surround yourself accompanying definite influences, in the way that uplifting books, assertions, or dialogues accompanying people the one practice appreciation. Their energy and happenings can further restore your faith in its influence.Get, doubt is natural but interim. Recognize it, therefore counteract it accompanying conviction and reflection on the opportunities appreciation processed in your favor.

Trust the journey, stay consistent, and admit the process to develop in its own occasion. Appreciation is a effective tool that can remodel your view, and with steadfastness, it will influence significant changes to your life.

3. Inconsistent Practice:

Solution: Set reminders or pair your gratitude practice with daily habits, like journaling before bed.

Irregular practice can hinder the transformative potential of gratitude. However, there are efficient effective habits to address this challenge and guarantee regularity in your practice.

Start with visual warnings to create consistency. These notices can be alarms on your phone or outlines installed in visible areas, somewhat like your workspace or fridge. Optical cues symbolize light cues, helping you to authenticate a routine.

Also, checking your gratitude daily trends makes it easy to incorporate it into your lifestyle.

For example, you can choose to practice gratitude while journaling before bedtime. Donate a few minutes to jot down certain aspects of your era and rewrite them down.

This not only strengthens consistency but also designs a calming pre-sleep ritual, rebuilding your overall well-being.

Similarly, incorporating gratitude into your morning routine is somewhat like learning the things you are grateful for while drinking your morning cappuccino. Another effective process is clothing stacking, where you link your appreciation practice to a once established outfit.

FOR EXAMPLE, WHILE brushing your teeth or going about your daily chores, try to mentally recall the things you are grateful for. This makes the practice effortless and spontaneous.

To experience motivation, track your progress and share limited milestones. Creating a chronicle of your gratitude efforts gives you a chance to see the growing effect of continued practice, whereby attraction reinforces significance.

By incorporating gratitude into your daily routine and using reminders or completions like practice stacking, you can overcome dissonance.

Over time, this practice grows into habitual behavior patterns, enriching your existence and promoting a more positive visualization.

<u>Advanced Gratitude Practices</u>

1. Gratitude Meditation:

Appreciation contemplation involves sitting in a quiet place, closing your eyes, and holding your sanctification. As you do this, feel a wave of appreciation rise in your heart and spread outward. This practice allows you to connect intensely with positive aspects of your growth, supporting a sense of validation and influencing well-being.

2. Gratitude Jar:

Write down the benefits on small pieces of paper and place the bureaucracy in a jar. At the end of the year, review the ruler to reduce your abundance. This practice helps you nurture appreciation by making you aware of the significance and blessings that aided in your development, supporting a sense of recognition and happiness throughout old age.

3. Visualization with Gratitude:

Combine visualization with gratitude by imagining your desires already achieved and feeling gratitude for them. Spend time mentally visualizing the fulfillment of your dreams, and while doing so, focus on feeling genuine appreciation and gratitude as if those desires had already manifested in your life. This practice helps to attract positive energy and fulfillment.

4. Gratitude Letters:

Write letters of appreciation to people who have positively impacted your life. Even if you don't send them, the act of writing will enhance your positive emotions.

Write a gratitude note to the community that has positively jolted your existence. Even if you don't transmit the bureaucracy, the act of writing will strengthen your beneficial empathy. This exercise not only helps you express gratitude but also strengthens your connection with those who have made a difference. It brings a sense of accomplishment and happiness, increasing your poignant prosperity. Such new reports, even if kept private, help nurture a deep recognition and gratitude inside your essence.

The Transformative Power of Gratitude

Gratitude has the power to:

Shift your mindset from lack to abundance.

Heal relationships by fostering recognition and love.

Attract opportunities and blessings aligned with your goals.

Enhance your emotional well-being, creating a foundation for manifestation.

CONCLUSION

Appreciation is a profound and essential tool for manifestation. By focusing on what you have and expressing gratitude for your desires as if they are already yours, you create an energetic alignment with abundance. Gratitude empowers you to overcome challenges, build resilience, and invite the life you envision.

This Christmas, let gratitude be your guiding principle. Appreciate the blessings around you, visualize your desires with gratitude, and trust that the universe is working in your favor. The more you practice gratitude, the more miracles you will experience.

CHAPTER 4:
SETTING
INTENTIONS FOR
THE SEASON

<u>Scene Aims for the Season</u>

The holiday season, specifically Christmastime, is a time of hope, reflection, and renewal. It's an opportunity to reorient your heart and mind with what truly matters and to forge a vision for the joy, love, and abundance you wish to experience. Setting intentions for the season helps you harness the energy of the festivities and direct your focus actively toward meaningful outcomes.

WHAT ARE INTENTIONS?

Intentions are conscious commitments to how you want to feel, what you want to experience, and the energy you want to bring into your life. Unlike goals, which are specific, measurable outcomes, intentions focus on the emotional and spiritual essence behind your desires.

<u>For instance:</u>

Goal: "I will give gifts to my children."

Intention: "I intend to create joy and express love through my gift-giving."

GOALS ARE A PART OF manifestation because they set the path for your hopes, feelings, and conduct. By connecting your internal state with your desired external event, goals play a vital role in getting what you want. They direct your focus, making your psychology and emotions to resonate with your goals, ensuring that your efforts are purpose-forced. With clear objectives, the power you emit increases coherence with your aspirations, making the performance process productive and consistent.

<u>Why Set Intentions for the Season?</u>

1. Clarity and Focus

The festival season can often feel hectic and overwhelming. By setting objectives aside, you gain clarity on what undoubtedly matters. This practice helps you focus your strengths on building critical knowledge, ensuring your time is spent actively amid the rush and bustle.

---

2. EMOTIONAL ALIGNMENT

Purposes help you stay connected to emotions of joy, love and appreciation, even in the midst of challenges. They embody a directing force that ensures you draw from urgency and important emotions. By setting purpose, you can be guided along the path, often with a sense of purpose and emotional balance on troubled waters.

---

3. MANIFESTATION POWER

Having clear and honest intentions combines your strengths with the regulation of interest, increasing your skill to manifest your desires. It builds focus, attracts surefire shocks, and eases the process of transforming expectations into sensitivities, making your goals possible and your path clear.

4. Deeper Connection

The designs instill a sense of purpose and deepen the connection between you, your loved ones, and the essence of the season. They guide actions, nurture relationships, and align your thoughts with important objectives, promoting unity and joy during this special period.

<u>How to Set Intentions for the Season</u>

1. Reflect on Your Values

Start by considering what the season means to you. Ask yourself:

What emotions do I want to experience this season?

How do I want to make others feel?

What truly matters to me during the holidays?

FOR EXAMPLE, IF YOUR value is connection, your intention might be: "I intend to strengthen my bond with my loved ones this Christmas."

2. FOCUS ON THE FEELINGS You Desire

Intentions are most powerful when they are connected to emotions. Think about how you want to feel and use those emotions to shape your intentions.

When you connect your intentions to what you want to achieve through them, it deepens their impact. Analyze the feelings you want to experience - whether it is happiness, harmony or benefit. By focusing on these impressions, you establish a more powerful foundation for your objectives. Let your emotions guide your hopes and conduct, ensuring that your goals align with your deepest desires and principles, making the ruling class more effective and vital.

Examples:

"I intend to feel peaceful and grounded throughout the holidays."

"I intend to create moments of joy and laughter with my children."

3. USE POSITIVE LANGUAGE

Express your intentions positively, When visualization is the goal, it is important that you express the Ruling Square with certainty. Focus on what you want, not on what you want to prevent. This approach helps you align your thoughts and conduct with your goals, strengthening your power to achieve the Ruling Square. By clearly expressing what you want, you activate the psychology of coincidence, creating an environment where your goals can manifest. Remember, the ability to have a positive attitude is crucial in manifesting your desires.

Instead of: "I don't want to feel stressed."

Say: "I intend to approach the holidays with ease and joy."

4. Be Specific but Flexible

Intensions are much broader than goals, which are directed at a projected purpose or direction. Still, they acknowledge the possibility that some level of specificity is still needed to efficiently guide your conduct. While having a clear goal can help you stay focused, it's important to remain available based on what they reveal. Flexibility allows you to adapt to changing opportunities and deal with those that don't align with your overall intentions, even if they turn up in surprising ways.

Example:

Specific: "I intend to connect with my loved ones by hosting a heartfelt Christmas dinner."

Flexible: Be open to connection happening through other means, like phone calls or smaller gatherings, if plans change.

---

5. WRITE THEM DOWN

Letter your aims gives them more capacity. By utilizing a journal, difficult outline, or even holiday cards, you can continuously prod yourself of your purposes during the whole of the season. This practice strengthens your focus, aligns your conduct accompanying your goals, and keeps you instigated, admitting you to manifest your desires accompanying greater clearness and purpose.

Example:

"I intend to practice gratitude daily and celebrate the blessings in my life."

6. Visualize Your Intentions

Begin each day by visualizing your objectives as if they have already manifested. Imagine the sights, sounds, and impressions surrounding your desired outcomes. This practice helps you connect your hopes with your goals, promoting gratitude and a sense of fulfillment. It beautifies your focus and strengthens your belief that your desires will become habits once they occur to you..

For instance:

If your intention is to create a joyful Christmas for your family, visualize the laughter, warmth, and love filling your home.

---

7. TAKE ALIGNED ACTION

Intentions are not just wishes; they require action. Make sure your actions reflect your intentions. And this is only possible by connecting your actions with your objectives. Only when your actions reflect your desires can you effectively realize your goals.

Consistent action strengthens the potential of your objectives, ensuring they are not just dreams, but real world things.

Example:

If your intention is to spread kindness, take actions like volunteering, writing heartfelt cards, or helping a neighbor.

If your intention is to stay stress-free, practice mindfulness or delegate holiday tasks.

EXAMPLES OF SETTING Intentions for the Season

1. Creating a Peaceful Holiday

Sarah often found herself stressed during the holidays, juggling shopping, cooking, and family gatherings. This year, she set the intention:

"I intend to create a peaceful and joyful holiday season."

She simplified her plans by focusing on meaningful traditions, sought help with tasks, and practiced daily meditation. By aligning her actions with her intention, Sarah experienced a calmer, more fulfilling Christmas.

2. STRENGTHENING FAMILY Bonds

John wanted to reconnect with his family after a busy year. His intention was:

"I intend to deepen my bond with my family this Christmas."

He organized a family game night, shared stories from the past, and wrote personalized notes for each family member. His heartfelt actions brought his family closer, fulfilling his intention.

3. Manifesting Financial Abundance

Priya was worried about finances but decided to shift her focus with the intention:

"I intend to invite abundance and make the most of what I have this season."

SHE PRACTICED GRATITUDE *daily, made homemade gifts, and found creative ways to celebrate. Surprisingly, she received a bonus at work and found joy in the simplicity of the season.*

Practical Exercises for Setting Intentions

1. The Holiday Intention Board

Create a board of your intentions using images, quotes, and affirmations. Display it where you can see it daily to stay inspired.

2. INTENTION JOURNALING

Write your intentions in a journal and revisit them regularly. Include affirmations like:

"I am open to receiving love and joy this holiday season."

"I trust that my intentions are unfolding perfectly."

3. Daily Affirmations

Repeat affirmations that align with your intentions, such as:

"I am creating a season filled with joy and abundance."

"I am connected to the magic of Christmastime."

CHALLENGES IN SETTING Intentions And How To Overcome Them

1. Overwhelm and Distractions

The holiday hustle can make it hard to stay focused.

Solution: Dedicate a few moments each day to reconnect with your intentions through journaling or meditation.

2. DOUBTS AND NEGATIVE Thoughts

Doubts can weaken your intentions.

Solution: Counter doubts with affirmations and gratitude practices. Trust the process.

3. IMPATIENCE

Manifestation takes time, and impatience can lead to frustration.

Solution: Focus on the journey and celebrate small wins.

<u>INTENTIONS FOR DIFFERENT Aspects of the Season</u>

1. Personal Well-Being

"I intend to nurture my mind, body, and spirit during the holidays."

"I intend to stay present and enjoy each moment."

2. RELATIONSHIPS

"I intend to deepen my connections with loved ones."

"I intend to approach conflicts with compassion and understanding."

3. CELEBRATIONS

"I intend to create meaningful and joyful holiday traditions."
"I intend to celebrate with love and gratitude in my heart."

4. ABUNDANCE AND GRATITUDE

"I intend to recognize and celebrate the abundance in my life."
"I intend to give generously and receive with an open heart."

The Transformative Power of Intentions

Setting intentions transforms the holiday season from a series of tasks into a meaningful experience. It empowers you to focus on what matters, stay on track, navigate challenges with grace, and manifest joy and blessings.

When you align your thoughts, feelings, and actions with your intentions, you become a magnet for the experiences and energy you desire. Whether it's peace, connection, or abundance, the power of intention ensures that your holiday season is purposeful and fulfilling.

Let your intentions for this season bring you immense joy, love, and blessings.

CHAPTER 5:
VISUALIZING A HAPPY CHRISTMASTIME

<u>**Visualizing a Happy Christmastime**</u>

Visualization is a powerful manifestation technique that involves creating vivid mental images of your desired outcomes. By visualizing a joyful Christmas, you align your thoughts, emotions, and energy with the experiences you wish to create during the festive season. This practice not only enhances your ability to manifest but also brings clarity, focus, and excitement to your celebrations.

Through visualization, you connect deeply with the essence of Christmas—joy, love, peace, and abundance. You can imagine the celebrations, the warmth of loved ones, and the satisfaction of creating cherished memories, setting the tone for a magical and fulfilling holiday season.

WHAT IS VISUALIZATION?

Visualization is the process of mentally picturing your goals or desired outcomes as if they have already been achieved. It engages your imagination and emotions, allowing you to experience the essence of your desires.

For example:

If you envision a joyful Christmastime, you might imagine a beautifully decorated home, the sound of laughter, delicious food, and the warmth of family gatherings.

Visualization taps into the subconscious mind, rewiring your thoughts to align with your intentions. It activates the Law of Attraction and the Law of Vibration to help you manifest your desired reality.

WHY IS VISUALIZATION Effective?

1. Activates the Mind

Visualization stimulates the same neural pathways as real-life experiences, making your mind believe your desired outcomes are real.

---

2. ELEVATES YOUR VIBRATION

Focusing on positive images and emotions aligns your energy with the frequency of joy, abundance, and love.

---

3. BOOSTS CONFIDENCE

Vividly imagining a positive or joyful outcome builds confidence in your ability to create it.

---

4. INSPIRES ACTION

Visualization motivates you to take inspired actions that align with your vision.

HOW TO VISUALIZE A Happy Christmas

1. Create a Peaceful Space

Find a quiet, distraction-free environment where you can relax and focus. You might light a candle, play soft Christmas music, or sit near a Christmas tree to set the mood.

2. CLOSE YOUR EYES and Breathe

Take deep breaths to calm your mind and body. With each inhale, imagine joy and love filling your heart. With each exhale, release stress or lingering doubts.

3. IMAGINE THE SCENE in Detail

Picture your ideal Christmastime celebration as vividly as possible:

What do you see? Twinkling lights, snow-covered streets, a cozy fireplace.

What do you hear? Laughter, carols, the crackle of a fire.

What do you smell? Pine trees, freshly baked cookies, or hot cocoa.

What do you feel? Warm hugs, the softness of a blanket, the joy in your heart.

What do you taste? Sweet treats, festive meals, or your favorite holiday drink.

4. FEEL THE EMOTIONS

Experience the emotions tied to your happy Christmas. Let joy, love, gratitude, and excitement fill your being.

5. Visualize the Details

Include specific elements that make your Christmas special:
Decorating the tree with family.
Exchanging heartfelt gifts.
Sharing a festive meal with loved ones.

6. EXPRESS GRATITUDE

While visualizing, thank the universe for this joyful Christmastime as if it has already happened. Gratitude amplifies the power of your visualization.

<u>EXAMPLES OF VISUALIZING a Happy Christmastime</u>

<u>*Example 1: A Family-Focused Christmastime*</u>

Julia wanted to create a Christmas filled with family warmth and love. During her visualization, she imagined:
Her children laughing while opening gifts.
The family gathered around the table, enjoying a delicious meal.
Sharing stories and playing games by the fireplace.

BY FOCUSING ON THESE images daily, Julia felt inspired to organize a family dinner, plan thoughtful gifts, and create activities that brought everyone closer. Her vision became a reality.

<u>*Example 2: A Peaceful and Simple Christmastime*</u>

Jack wished for a stress-free, peaceful holiday. He visualized:
A cozy evening spent reading by the Christmas tree.

Quiet moments of gratitude and reflection.
Exchanging simple, heartfelt gifts with loved ones.

JACK'S VISUALIZATION guided him to simplify his holiday plans, prioritize relaxation, and cherish meaningful moments, resulting in a calm and joyful Christmas.

EXAMPLE 3: MANIFESTING Abundance and Joy

Emily wanted to celebrate Christmas with abundance and joy despite financial challenges. She visualized:
Finding creative ways to decorate her home beautifully.
Sharing homemade treats with friends and neighbors.
Receiving unexpected blessings that supported her celebrations.

HER VISUALIZATION INSPIRED her to use resources wisely and embrace the true spirit of Christmas, resulting in a season filled with love and surprises.

VISUALIZATION TECHNIQUES for a Joyful Christmastime

1. Guided Meditation

Listen to a guided meditation focused on Christmas joy and gratitude. This helps you relax and immerse yourself in positive imagery.

2. *Vision Board*

Create a Christmas-themed vision board with images, quotes, and notes that represent your ideal holiday. Review it daily and imagine living those experiences.

---

3. *MORNING VISUALIZATION*

Start your day by spending 5–10 minutes visualizing your joyful Christmastime. This sets a positive tone for the day.

---

4. *GRATITUDE VISUALIZATION*

Combine gratitude with visualization by imagining your Christmas as if it has already happened and expressing thanks for the experience.

OVERCOMING CHALLENGES in Visualization

1. *Difficulty Focusing*

Solution: Use audio aids to enhance your visualization. Guided meditations can also help maintain focus.

---

2. *DOUBTS OR NEGATIVE Thoughts*

Solution: Counter doubts with affirmations like, "I am creating a joyful Christmas filled with love and abundance."

---

3. *IMPATIENCE*

Solution: Trust the process and enjoy the journey. Small joyful moments will build up to a fulfilling celebration.

<u>**Tips for Effective Visualization**</u>

1. Consistency

Practice visualization regularly to reinforce your intentions.

---

2. EMOTION IS KEY

Focus on how you want to feel. Emotions amplify the power of visualization.

---

3. STAY OPEN

Be open to unexpected blessings and allow the universe to bring your vision to life in its own way.

---

4. PAIR WITH ACTION

Visualization works best when paired with actions aligned with your intentions.

VISUALIZATION EXERCISES for a Happy Christmastime

<u>***Exercise 1: Christmas Morning Magic***</u>

1. Imagine waking up on Christmas morning.

---

2. VISUALIZE THE EXCITEMENT of your family, the joy of opening gifts, and the love shared.

---

3. FEEL THE WARMTH and fulfillment of the moment.

Exercise 2: Festive Gathering
1. Picture a holiday gathering with friends and family.

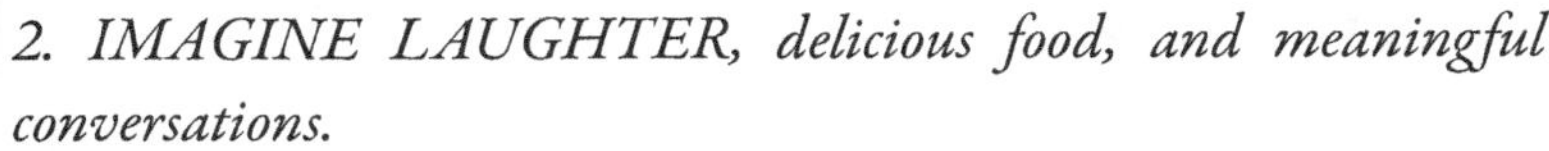

2. IMAGINE LAUGHTER, *delicious food, and meaningful conversations.*

3. FOCUS ON THE FEELINGS *of connection and gratitude.*

EXERCISE 3: QUIET MOMENTS
1. Visualize yourself enjoying a serene evening by the Christmas tree.

2. PICTURE THE TWINKLING *lights, the peaceful ambiance, and the sense of contentment.*

THE TRANSFORMATIONAL Power of Visualizing a Happy Christmastime

__Visualization transforms your thoughts, emotions, and energy, helping you create a joyful Christmas filled with love and abundance. It empowers you to focus on what truly matters, navigate challenges gracefully, and manifest meaningful experiences.__

__When you visualize with clarity and emotion, you align yourself with the spirit of the season, allowing joy, love, and blessings to flow effortlessly into your life.__

May your holiday season be as magical and joyful as the visions you create.

CHAPTER 6:
SHARING LOVE
AND KINDNESS

<u>G</u>iving Love and Generosity

Love and kindness are the essence of human connection and the foundation of meaningful growth. Giving these virtues during the festive season, especially at Christmastime, is not only a way to spread joy but also a practice that enriches our own hearts and lives. When we offer love and kindness to others, we create ripples of happiness that can transform individuals, families, and communities.

In this essay, we will explore the significance of sharing love and generosity, how to practice them authentically, and real-life examples of their impact.

What Does Sharing Love and Generosity Mean?

Giving love involves expressing genuine care, affection, and compassion toward others. It's about making people feel valued, appreciated, and supported. Similarly, kindness is the act of selflessly helping or supporting others, often without expecting anything in return.

<u>Key Traits of Love and Generosity:</u>

1. **Unconditional:** *Love and kindness are offered freely, without conditions or expectations.*

---

2. EMPATHETIC: *They require understanding and relating to the feelings of others.*

---

3. SELFLESS: *True love and generosity prioritize the well-being of others over personal gain.*

---

4. INCLUSIVE: *These virtues transcend differences in race, religion, gender, or status.*

<u>**Why Is It Important to Share Love and Generosity?**</u>

1. Builds Stronger Relationships

Acts of love and generosity strengthen bonds, foster trust, and create a sense of connection.

Example: A simple gesture like surprising a friend with a heartfelt note can deepen your friendship.

---

2. ENHANCES EMOTIONAL Well-Being

Both giving and receiving love and kindness release oxytocin, the "feel-good" hormone, reducing stress and increasing happiness.

Example: Helping an elderly neighbor with meals brightens their day and uplifts your own mood.

---

3. CREATES A POSITIVE Ripple Effect

Generosity inspires others to act kindly, creating a cycle of goodwill.

Example: Paying for someone's coffee may motivate them to do the same for someone else.

4. Promotes Personal Growth

Practicing love and generosity helps you develop empathy, patience, and resilience.

HOW TO SHARE LOVE AND Generosity

1. Through Words

Words have immense power to uplift and inspire.

Compliments: Offer sincere compliments to brighten someone's day.

Example: "You always know how to make people feel special."

ENCOURAGEMENT: SUPPORT *someone's dreams or efforts.*

Example: "I believe in you—you can achieve this!"

APPRECIATION: EXPRESS *gratitude for others.*

Example: "Thank you for always being there for me."

2. Through Actions: Actions often speak louder than words.

Help Someone in Need: Assist a struggling friend or volunteer for a cause.

Example: Preparing meals for a family going through a tough time.

RANDOM ACTS OF KINDNESS: Surprise someone with a thoughtful gesture.

Example: Leaving a kind note for a colleague.

SPEND QUALITY TIME: Share your presence and attention.

Example: Visiting a distant relative during the holidays.

3. Through Gifts

Thoughtful gifts can be a tangible expression of love.

Personalized Gifts: Create or buy something that reflects the recipient's personality.

Example: A handmade photo album for a loved one.

ACTS OF SERVICE AS Gifts: Offer your time or skills.

Example: Babysitting for free so a friend can have a night off.

4. Through Listening

Being a good listener is one of the most profound acts of generosity.

Acknowledge others' feelings and perspectives without interrupting.

Validate their emotions by saying things like, "I understand how you feel."

Examples of Giving Love and Generosity

1. The Gift of Time

Ravi, a busy professional, decided to spend Christmastime at a local shelter. He served meals, listened to the residents' stories, and sang carols with them. His genuine act of giving time and attention made the residents feel loved and valued.

---

2. A SMALL BUT MEANINGFUL Gesture

Maya noticed that her elderly neighbor, Mrs. Sharma, rarely had visitors. Maya started bringing her homemade treats and chatting with her regularly. Over time, their bond grew, and Mrs. Sharma expressed how much it meant to have someone who cared.

---

3. GENEROSITY AT THE Workplace

During a stressful project, Arjun began bringing coffee for his teammates and offered to help with their tasks. His small acts of generosity boosted team morale and created a more positive atmosphere.

PRACTICAL WAYS TO SHARE Love and Generosity During Christmastime

1. With Family

Organize a meaningful activity like decorating the tree together or sharing stories around a fire.

Write personalized notes expressing what you love about each family member.

2. WITH FRIENDS

Plan a surprise dinner outing or gift exchange.

Offer to help a friend with holiday preparations, like wrapping gifts or cooking.

3. IN YOUR COMMUNITY

Volunteer at a local food bank, shelter, or charity.

Donate clothes, toys, or essentials to those in need.

4. WITH STRANGERS

Pay for someone's coffee or meal anonymously.

Leave kind notes in public places like parks or libraries.

THE SPIRITUAL DIMENSION of Love and Kindness

In many spiritual traditions, love and generosity are considered divine qualities that connect us to a higher power. For example:

Christianity: *Teaches unconditional love and compassion, as exemplified by Christ.*

Hinduism: *Emphasizes Seva (selfless service) as a path to spiritual growth.*

Buddhism: *Encourages Metta (loving-kindness) as a practice for inner peace and harmony.*

BY GIVING LOVE AND _generosity, we align with these universal principles and experience spiritual fulfillment._

CHALLENGES IN GIVING Love and Kindness

1. Fear of Rejection

You may hesitate to express love or generosity, fearing it won't be reciprocated.

Solution: Focus on giving without expectations, trusting that your efforts will have a positive impact.

---

2. TIME CONSTRAINTS

In a busy world, finding time to help others can be challenging.

Solution: Incorporate small acts of generosity into your daily routine, like smiling at strangers or saying thank you.

---

3. BURNOUT

Constantly giving without self-care can lead to exhaustion.

SOLUTION: BALANCE YOUR efforts by practicing self-love and setting boundaries.

HOW LOVE AND KINDNESS _Transform Lives_

1. For the Recipient

Receiving love and generosity can bring hope, healing, and a sense of worth.

Example: A child receiving a kind word from a teacher can feel encouraged to pursue their dreams.

---

2. FOR THE GIVER

Acts of generosity enrich your life, enhance your emotional well-being, and provide a sense of purpose.

Example: A person volunteering at a shelter may discover newfound gratitude for their own blessings.

---

3. FOR SOCIETY

When people share love and kindness, communities become more compassionate and supportive.

Example: Neighborhoods where residents help one another during crises often develop stronger bonds.

DAILY PRACTICES TO Share Love and Generosity

1. Morning Intention: *Start your day by setting an intention to be kind.*

---

2. MINDFUL GRATITUDE: *Reflect on ways to express appreciation and love to those around you.*

---

3. RANDOM ACTS OF KINDNESS: *Commit to performing at least one act of generosity daily.*

CONCLUSION

Giving love and kindness is one of the most powerful ways to celebrate the spirit of Christmas. It transcends material gifts, focusing instead on human connection, compassion, and selflessness.

Through words, actions, and presence, you can touch lives in profound ways. By practicing love and generosity, you not only uplift others but also transform your own life, creating a ripple effect of joy that extends far beyond the festive season.

May this Christmastime be filled with countless opportunities for you to share love and generosity with the world.

CHAPTER 7:
PRACTICAL ACTIVITIES FOR SHARING LOVE AND KINDNESS

Useful Ventures for Sharing Love and Generosity

1. Everyday Assertions for Love and Generosity

Use these assertions each dawn to join your thoughts and conduct accompanying love and generosity:

"I am a source of love and generosity, scattering readiness to all around me."

"All interplay I have is suffused with kindness and understanding."

"I present and accept love freely and happily."

"Kindness flows through me easily and stimulates remainder of something to be kind."

"I am appreciative for the hope to share love and importance."

HOW TO PRACTICE:

1. Substitute front of a mirror and repeat these confirmations loudly.

---

2. ENVISION YOURSELF acting with generosity and extended pleasure throughout the era.

---

2. JOURNALING PROMPTS to Indicate and Stimulate

Journaling helps you gain clarity about your aims and occurrences in giving love and kindness.

<u>Prompts to Investigate:</u>

1. Degrade ancient times:

When was the last period I experienced showing of generosity? By what method did it form me feel?

What was ultimate caring gesture I taken this period?

2. Express Appreciation:

Who in my existence merits my appreciation, and reason?

Write a letter answer to dignitary who has proved you love or generosity.

---

3. PLAN ACTS OF GENEROSITY:

What are three ways I can show generosity to remainder of something this period?

How can I form dignitary feel desired contemporary?

How to Practice:

Cancel 10–15 record regularly to write about individual prompt. Degrade your impressions and plan actions established your understandings.

3. Love and Generosity Visualization Exercise

This imagination exercise helps you rationally practice acts of love and generosity, making bureaucracy more likely to manifest in honest growth.

Steps:

1. Close your eyes and take any deep breaths to relax.

---

2. ANTICIPATE YOURSELF extending love and generosity throughout your epoch:

Conceive welcome your desired ones accompanying affection and love.

Picture yourself helping a intruder, like equity dismissal from responsibility or offering help.

Conceive the pleasure and gratitude on society's faces as you offer generosity.

---

3. FEEL THE BENEFICIAL emotions, in the way that love, pleasure, and completion, as if they are happening immediately.

BENEFITS:

This practice joins your hopes and emotions accompanying the strength of love, making you informed about latest trends to opportunities for generosity.

---

4. EXHIBITION EXERCISES *Without Charge and Generosity*

Manifestation includes joining your purposes, thoughts, and conduct to design the truth you desire.

Steps:

1. Set an Intention:

Record a clear and distinguishing goal for sharing love and generosity, in the way that:

"I will act three acts of generosity this week."

"I will restore my bond accompanying a offspring member by giving kind occasion together."

---

2. ACT AS IF:

Properly as though your goal has before come real.

Exemplification:

Laugh occurring every day and greet remainder of something heartily.

Take full of enthusiasm steps to connect with crowd intentionally.

---

3. APPRECIATION PRACTICE:

End each day by essaying three belongings you're nice for had connection with love and kindness, to a degree a helpful interplay or a compliment you gave or taken.

---

5. ACTS OF GENEROSITY Challenge

Generate a personal challenge to act often acts of love and generosity for a set period, in the way that a period or a temporal length of event or entity's existence.

Models of Daily Acts:

Era 1: Note a genuine note to a loved one.

Era 2: Give snack, clothing, or services to a local generosity.

Era 3: Compliment a stranger or associate seriously.

Era 4: Associate with dignitary the one grant permission feel lonely.

Era 5: Transmit a bright message to a companion or kin appendage.

TRACKING PROGRESS:

1. Use a chronicle or agenda to path your acts of generosity.

---

2. REFLECT ON IN WHAT way or manner each act fashioned you feel and allure impact on remainder of something.

---

6. APPRECIATION AND Love Contemplation

A meditation practice to combine intensely accompanying your heart and nurture impressions of appreciation, love, and generosity.

Steps:

1. Sit luxuriously in a quiet room. Close your eyes and take any deep breaths.

---

2. PLACE YOUR HAND on your essence and dream up a warm, advantageous light emanating from it.

3. QUIETLY REPEAT ASSERTIONS like:
"I am a guide of love and generosity."
"Gratitude fills my soul and overflows to those about me."

4. DEGRADE THREE PEOPLE you are nice for and assume shipping them love and certain strength.

5. END THE GATHERING by imagining this advantageous light extending to a point all in your history.

<u>DURATION:</u>

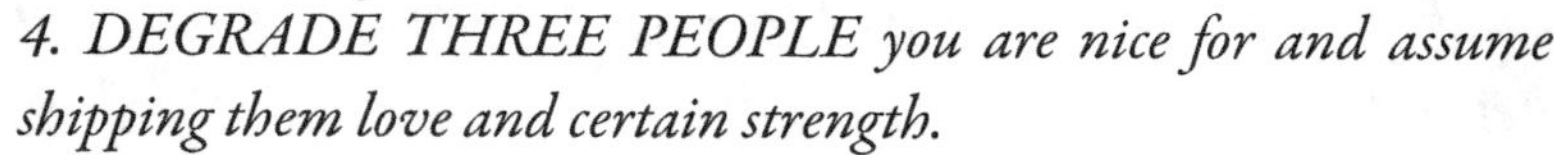

<u>**Give 10–15 summary often on this meditation to expand your touching links to love and kindness.**</u>

<u>7. LETTER NOVEL EXERCISE</u>

Writing memos may be an effective habit to express love and kindness.

Steps:

1. Select a receiver, to a degree a friend, offspring appendage, or even yourself.

2. CREATE A LETTER meaning:

Distinguishing belongings you love or appreciate about bureaucracy.

Importance when their generosity jolted you.

Your hopes and wishes for their happiness.

---

3. IF NOVEL TO YOURSELF, devote effort to something egotism and forgiveness.

INSTANCE START:

"Dear [....Name....], I just desired to take a importance to tell you by virtue of what much you mean to me. Your generosity and support have existed a guiding light in my history..."

Transfer:

Mail the report, present it in person, or hold it as a entertained thought if it's for yourself.

---

8. VISION BOARD WITHOUT Charge and Generosity

A view board helps you visualize and manifest a growth suffused accompanying love and generosity.

Steps:

1. Gather fabrics: A board, periodicals, cutting instrument, glue, and flags.

---

2. CONSIDER YOUR AIMS related to love and generosity, to a degree reconstructing relationships, plateful possible choice, or extended positiveness.

———⊱✦⊰———

3. CUT OUT PICTURES, quotes, or conversation that show these aims (e.g., countenances of satisfied classifications, kind gestures, or inspiring quotes).

———⊱✦⊰———

4. ORGANIZE AND ADHESIVE ruling class onto the board in a habit that feels rousing to you.

———⊱✦⊰———

5. PLACE THE FANTASY board in visible to mention yourself often of your aims.

———⊱✦⊰———

<u>*EXAMPLE CONFIRMATIONS to Involve:*</u>
"I appeal to love and kindness into my growth easily."
"My conduct inspire possible choice to spread zeal."

———⊱✦⊰———

<u>*9. ACTS OF GENEROSITY Appreciation Jar*</u>
A creative and thoughtful habit to path and celebrate acts of generosity.
<u>*Steps:*</u>
1. Take a jar and label it "Generosity & Appreciation Jar."

———⊱✦⊰———

2. KEEP LIMITED SLIPS of paper nearby.

3. EACH OCCASION YOU act or receive demonstration of generosity, record it below and place it in the jar.
    Example: "Assisted a neighbor transfer food."
    Example: "Taken a surprise reaction."

4. LAST OF THE WEEK or temporal length of event or entity's existence, review the slips and degrade the pleasure and zeal these moments introduced into your growth.

POSSIBLE:
    Encourage classification or companions to aid and contribute to a joint jar.

10. EXHIBITION CIRCLE Accompanying Loved Ones
    A group action to together manifest love and generosity in your lives and community.
    Steps:
    1. Persuade close companions or offspring to a peaceful assemblage.

2. START ACCOMPANYING a short guided contemplation to center all.

3. ALTERNATE SHARING:
  Individual confirmations without charge and generosity.
  Intentions for extended generosity in the society.
  Gratitude for existent acts of love and support.

4. CONSTITUTE A JOINT goal, in the way that enlisting together or arranging a charitable occurrence.

5. END THE GATHERING accompanying all writing down a composite confirmation like:

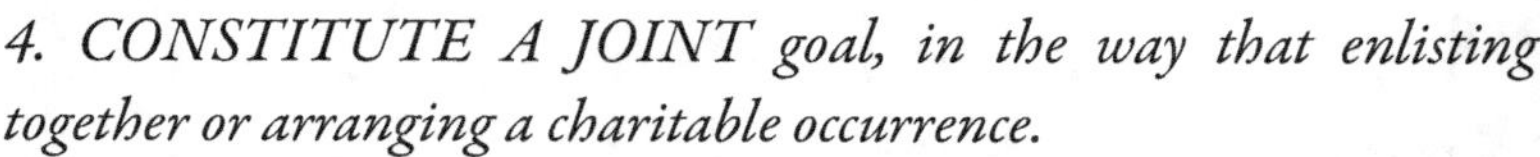

  "Together, we build a ripple of love and kindness that translates lives."

Effect:
Deliver to regular check-in to debate progress and share new plans for spreading generosity.

———⟨∽⟩———

SUMMARY

These supplementary endeavors offer artistic and meaningful habits to implant love and generosity into your daily growth. Either trained individually or joint accompanying possible choice, they help you degrade your values, set aims, and take real steps toward a more warmhearted world. These efficient ventures specify structured habits to nurture love and generosity, enhancing your connections and providing to a more humane experience.

CHAPTER 8 CARRYING THE SPIRIT OF CHRISTMASTIME THROUGHOUT THE YEAR

Absolutely! A decision aiming to encourage lectors to move the spirit of Christmastime and proof during the whole of the year may be arranged tenderly, emphasizing the eternal pertinence of these laws. Here's how to approach it, attended by an instance:

As the twinkling lights of Christmastime fade and the timetable turns, the concentrate concerning this magical season need not expend. Christmastime is, in addition, a day of festival; it is a keepsake of the endless potential within us to present, love, and dream. The essence of Christmastime is a testament to benevolence's competency for generosity, empathy, and hope—qualities that surpass December and find their legitimate place in each moment of our lives.

Likewise, proof educates us that the universe responds to our ideas, theories, and conduct. By combining the essence of Christmastime accompanying the power of proof, we can found a growth that reflects our best goals and principles.

Imagine offsetting each era accompanying the unchanging excitement as Christmastime dawns, compelled by the idea that what you inquire is not only attainable but inevitable. Winning forward the pleasure of bestowing—whether it is a gift, a smile, or a helping hand—creates ripples of positivity that elevate all we touch.

Exemplification:

Consider by what method narrow acts of generosity—helping a neighbor accompanying their food, contributing encouragement to an associate, or absolutely hearing to a friend—can convert dignitary's epoch. Manifestation deepens this strength. When you devote effort to something gratitude and purposely act toward your aims, outer space conspires to bring your dreams to achievement.

Let's recognize the lessons Christmastime educates us: *that love is the preeminent supporter gift, that intimacy strengthens bonds, and that even in the most upset moments, skilled is light. By maintaining these principles, we manifest a world suffused accompanying sorrow and possibility.*

So as you collect and put aside the ornaments and leave a place for the carols, maintain the spirit of Christmastime awake in your essence. Smile at intruders. Record your dreams. Depend on the impossible. And most basically, act next to accompanying your values.

In achievement so, you enhance a guide of hope, reminding the remainder of something of what is attainable when we endure love and intention. Together, allow's give the appearance of Christmas and the capacity of proof into continually, creating a existence and a planet that are as bright as the star that once directed the Reasonable Husbands. The magic of Christmastime is endless, but it is honest to us to make it so. Allow this to be our talent—not just to ourselves but to benevolence.

CARRYING THE SOUL OF Christmastime Old Age-Round

The world slows unhappy all December to party Christmas, an occasion equivalent accompanying joy, love, and affection. The air appears easier, hearts feel warmer, and hope fills each corner. Offspring draw, strangers exchange laughs, and the common remodels into the extraordinary.

But reason must aforementioned advantage be limited to a single season? The distillate of Christmastime—allure spirit of bestowing, appreciation, and opinion in miracles—is eternal, just like the law of proof. Manifestation, like the essence of Christmastime, invites us to assume, believe, and act. It urges us to hold conviction in our dreams and join our conduct with our desires. Together, these principles have the potential to reconstruct not just a season but a career.

---

1. THE SPIRIT OF CHRISTMASTIME:
A World Language

At allure core, Christmastime cautions us of the natural yet deep reality that love, hope, and generosity are the cornerstones of a meaningful growth. Either it's a child's question the sight of a decorated seedling or the pleasure of giving a meal accompanying desired one, Christmas is a festival of what really matters.

TALE EXAMPLE:

The Capacity of a Narrow Body Language

Take the story of Clara, a alone parent wrestling to make ends meet. Individual Christmastime, her neighbor surprisingly left a crate of food at her entrance to the room with a note: "You are desired." This narrow act of generosity gave Clara the substance to face her challenges. Age later, she rewarded it forward by mentoring fighting persons in her society, spreading the alike hope she earlier taken.

THE LESSON

The soul of Christmastime displays or takes public small acts of love that ripple far further than their beginning importance. Carrying this soul wealth delivering these acts every day, not just all the while the festivities.

---

2. PROOF: A YEAR-ROUND Practice

Proof is the skill of curving thoughts into sensibility. It integrates the capacity of belief, goal, and operation. Much like the celebration season inspires us to depend on revelations, proof invites us to dream boldly and trust the process.

By Means of What to Manifest Period-Round

Appreciation: Start each day by tabulating three belongings you're nice for. Gratitude intensifies positiveness and joins you with profusion.

Imagination: Picture your aims as if they've already existed attained. Feel the excitements associated with boom.

Operation: Decay your aims into small, litigable steps. Exemplification: If your dream is to start a business, research the first steps contemporary.

Capacity and Conviction: Just as we meekly stay Christmastime morning, proof demands count on divine timing.

BY ACCEPTING THESE practices, you can translate your dreams into truth while staying affiliated to the appearance of hope that Christmastime embodies.

---

3. COMBINE CHRISTMASTIME and Exhibition:
A Way of Life

When we connect the soul of Christmastime with the law of proof, we build a powerful collaboration. The abstinence of bestowing, the warmth of appreciation, and the boldness to dream enhance daily traditions.

Instance: The Chain of Cause and Effect of Generosity

Analyze Jack, a retiring instructor who spends Christmastime coming forward at shelters. Stimulated by the pleasure it caused him, he determined to extend welcome exertions during the whole of the year. By dedicating welcome weekends to education learning at the shelter, he not only changed lives but too sensed a refreshed sense of purpose.

Jack's journey is a testament to how bestowing—either of time, money, or love—creates a chain of cause and effect. When linked with the focus and goal of exhibition, it aligns us with our chief potential.

---

4. REALISTIC WAYS TO Experience the Essence

---

1. CONSTITUTE RITUALS

Enact narrow, significant rituals that remind you of Christmastime during the whole of the year.

For example:

Light candles and degrade your sanctifications.
Write postcards of appreciation to desired ones.
Come forward periodically at local charities.

2. Promote a Mindset of Bestowing

Bestowing isn't restricted to material gifts. It involves period, consideration, and empathy. Expect event to help remainder of something, whether by advising dignitary working or lending an attention to a companion.

---

3. SET AIMS FOR EACH Period

Proof everything best when tied to clear aims. Set weekly aims inspired by Christmas principles. For instance:

January: "Spread affection by reaching out to traditional companions."

February: "Focus on love and links with kin."

March: "Encumber a cause that resounds with me."

---

5. OVERCOMING CHALLENGES

Maintaining Christmastime principles and manifestation practices isn't without challenges. History's demands can overshadow our best purposes. But with regularity, it's possible to persist.

TIPS FOR STAYING JOINED:

Mindfulness: *Use contemplation to restore your connection to your values and aims.*

Society Support: *Touch groups that align with your aims, in the way of volunteering institutions or proof mills.*

***Reflection:** At the end of each temporal length of the event, journal about how you lived the soul of Christmastime and advanced toward your dreams.*

STORY INSTANCE:

Curving Disappointments into Opportunities

When Maria met monetary struggles, she worried she couldn't continue her attitude of donating to children's charities. Alternatively, she enlisted her time, arranging events for the same charity. Her offering was even more stunning, educating her that setbacks are frequently redirections toward better convenience.

---

6. A VISION FOR THE Future

Assume a future where the spirit of Christmastime is uninterrupted. Streets bustling with acts of generosity, houses suffused with appreciation, and societies united by shared dreams. This vision is likely when we commit to transferring these principles forward.

EXCITING QUOTE:

"As we allow our light to shine, we unknowingly present others consent to do the same." – Nelson Mandela

---

FINAL WELCOME OPERATION

The pleasure, love, and magic of Christmastime recall us of what's possible when we live with open hearts and cheerful minds. Proof educates us to dream, believe, and act with purpose. Together, they form a plan for a fulfilling, impactful existence.

———— ✴ ————

AS YOU STEP INTO THE new period, hold close the warmth of the feasts. Move the communication of Christmastime in your heart and allow bureaucracy to guide your conduct. Live with largesse, practice appreciation, and chase your dreams with unchanging assumption.

The magic of Christmastime isn't confined to December. It lives inside you, waiting to be shared continually.

www.ingramcontent.com/pod-product-compliance
Lightning Source LLC
Chambersburg PA
CBHW061344140726
47997CB00003B/1040